The ~~10~~ 11 Commandments of Real Estate Sales

By Chuck Whitehead

Table of Contents

Introduction

From the outside, the real estate business looks like easy money. Sit some floor time or a few open houses and the clients and commissions will come rolling in. The next thing you know, you're on a yacht surrounded by half-naked models or maybe some hot cabana boys. This sounds like a great gig! Especially, for those who are working dead-end jobs. Who wouldn't want to be their own boss? But one of the biggest reasons why people fail in real estate is they forget being your own boss also means that you must "BE" your own boss. You must do what a boss does: give yourself the motivation, direction, focus, action plan, and the accountability you need for success.

My Story

I have been in real estate for a little over 23 years. I did not originally intend to get into real estate. Like most people, I ended up here. After high school, I worked odd jobs ranging from fast food, a grocery store box boy, and a weekend secretary at a local real estate company. During my time at the real estate company, I paid $100 to go to real estate school. I spent another $200 to get my license. Being 19, I lacked the confidence to make a run at a real estate sales career and went on to work many other retail jobs.

In my search for success, I enrolled in community college, transferred to a four-year college and earned a bachelor's degree in public service. Eventually, I earned a master's degree in public administration from University of Southern California (USC). All the while, accumulating nearly $100,000 in student-loan debt.

After graduation, I called Margaret, the broker I worked for as a secretary during my college years and asked her if I could borrow their office computer and printer. I was excited to update my resume and proudly add USC to my education section. At that point in my life, I was shooting for what I then considered loftier goals – President of the United States (or at least a city manager).

Real estate was the furthest thing from my mind. However, the direction of my life changed. While updating my resume, a young couple wandered into the office looking to buy a home. As there were no agents in the office at the time, Margaret asked me if I could show them a few properties. She printed 6 listings, loaned me the keys to her car, and the rest was history. By that afternoon, we had an accepted offer and I was 30 days away from my first commission.

> **"Little did I know that the $100,000 in students I had borrowed for my education would net me almost zero income, while the $300 I had invested in a real estate license at 19 would turn out to make me millions in commission dollars, and provide me with an exciting and enriching lifelong career."**

Since the day I sold Dan and Heather that first home, I have sold over $200,000,000 in properties, built 15 homes, rehabbed and flipped over 100 properties, and invested in residential and commercial income property. Now I'm a partner in my own brokerage with nearly 300 amazing agents.

Our top ten agents will yield close to $400,000 in commission, with our top three each exceeding $1,000,000 in commissions.

In my 23 years in real estate sales, I have met thousands of agents and seen many talented people fail and have to return to their previous careers. The fact is, 70% of people who enter the real estate business leave it within the first 18 months. To make matters even worse, of those who do make it, only a select few will enjoy any real financial success.

Knowing this, the big question we need to address is:

"What distinguishes those who achieve financial success from the vast number of failed agents?"

It is not a difficult question to answer for the top agent. If you asked most top agents, they will tell you, **"success or failure in real estate sales is based on an agent's ability to create and cultivate leads."**

Top agents will also tell you that there are some very basic lead generation techniques that need to be part of EVERY AGENTS arsenal. Success in this business is not some magical mystery. It is a simple equation: **Lead Generation = Success**. Thus, it is often a waste of money to invest in the newest outside the box real estate programs. Success is about using the lead generation techniques already being utilized by successful real estate agents across the country. These techniques have a track record of success.

This book shares my Eleven Commandments of Real Estate Sales, which if embraced, will make you millions of dollars in commissions and enrich your life along the way. If followed, these commandments WILL lead you to your own financial and career heaven.

COMMANDMENT 1

Become a Walking, Talking Billboard

Being social is a major component of lead generation. The first step to being social is to BE
INVOLVED WITH SOMETHING. Whether you
are active in your church, your kid's sports, golf
groups, pet shelters, or a specific charity, I
encourage you to become even more involved.
Get out there and meet people!

We all have personal passions and interests
and *right now* is a perfect time to embrace them.
My advice is to not just be a member, but to be a
leader. For example, if your kids play sports, be
the team mom or dad. Send out the reminders,
be the point of communication. Get the parents'

phone numbers, emails, and other contact information. Be responsible for your group's communication methods where you can sign off with your real estate email. Or find some other position that puts you in a high-profile role.

"Real estate is one of the few careers where we get paid to be social. Everything we do and everywhere we go is an opportunity to find someone who may eventually buy or sell!"

Your responsibility in your organization and in everything you do is to get known. Whether you sponsor events, offer raffle drawings or prizes, DO SOMETHING! If you are afraid to appear too pushy by giving back through your efforts or sponsorships, get over it.

Once you have decided to engage in being social, one of the most cost-effective lead generation tools is to always wear company apparel and/or your name tag. So many real estate agents fight this. Admittedly, it can feel embarrassing at first to wear apparel or a name tag at a Parent Teacher Association meeting, or out shopping, or at lunch. One way to view this, famous people and athletes are paid to wear their brands of business in public. By wearing your real estate brand in public, I guarantee it will pay you as well.

Our agents have listed and sold homes to the Kohl's cashier, waiters and waitresses, and hundreds of other clients off of our apparel and name tags alone.

Remember the conversation about overcoming our fears? You need to wear your name tag as often as possible. You should keep your name tag in your car cup holder. Never take it off during daylight hours, even when you are at your child's sporting event, walking around in the grocery store, or shopping at the mall. You will find people breaking their neck to read your name tag. Don't be shy, own it.

In addition to the name tag, I am a huge fan of the people who wrap and brand their vehicles. My top agents, who each make well over $700,000 per year, have their cars wrapped. Wherever they drive, they are clearly advertising, "We sell homes!", and it is tax deductible! If you are not ready to spend the money to wrap your car, you need to at least buy car magnets for it. Your job is to let everyone know what you do. We've had multiple sales from neighbors who had no idea that the person living next door was an agent until they saw the car branding.

Branding yourself with a memorable name or characterization can be a huge benefit to your business. **Is your name and branding unique and**

memorable? My top agents for the last few years have been Mike and Robyn Zingg. Everyone in our community knows them as the "Super Zinggs". Most of their advertisements have them in superhero costumes with a Z for Zingg on their chests. When the Zinggs go to parades or community events, they wear their costumes and throw Hostess Zingers to the kids.

They have made tens of millions of dollars in commissions using this branding. With that kind of return, I am close to buying a white cape, putting on some tights, and changing my name to "Super Whitehead" (although it doesn't have quite the same ring).

Finally, it is important to remember that wearing apparel or branding, besides being a great way to advertise what you do, also opens the door to great real estate conversations. These conversations are a great opportunity to generate leads, so don't overlook their importance. Always be enthusiastic in your response about your job. When you are asked about your name tag, shirt, or car, be sure to have an answer and a business card at the ready to give out. **Most importantly, be ready to collect their contact information!**

COMMANDMENT 2

Run a "Kickass" Open House

The open house without a doubt, is the quickest and best way to earn a paycheck in real estate. It is also the cheapest and most effective source of standing face-to-face with live people who may be looking to buy or sell a home.

One of the most successful agents I know, has a very simple business plan. He sits open houses 4 days per week, and by doing this, he closes roughly 6 transactions per month. Not a bad business plan! Also, for many of the most successful team models, a minimum of 1 open house per week is required of team members.

It is AMAZING how many closings are the powerful result of a well-executed open house.

Creating a well-executed open house is simple. Below are 9 powerful tips that people need to follow to optimize the success of their open house.

1. The 5/5/10 Rule:

Before you begin the open house, create "personalized to you" open house flyers and knock on the 5 doors to the left of the house, on the 5 doors to the right, then the 10 neighbors across the street. Invite them to stop by. These neighbors likely have friends and family looking to move to the area, but more importantly, they may be interested in buying or selling. At the least, if the conversation goes well, you can add them to your potential client pool (PCP).

2. *Signage and Location:*

The number of signs and location of the open house is extremely important. A high profile, easy to find location is necessary for a successful open house. No one is going to the Sahara Desert, unless you build some pyramids. In addition, the importance of the number of signs should not be neglected. The number of signs you put out will generally match the number of people you can expect. For example, 3 signs should equal 3 groups, while 20 signs should draw in 20 groups. Also, balloons or something to draw attention to the signs is a good idea. It will add to the "bang-for-the-buck" of each sign (Helium is a real estate agent's best friend for a successful open house).

3. The Root Beer Float Method:

Having something to serve potential walk-ins like root beer floats can often break the ice with potential clients. Normally, the agents will start with the standard line of "Welcome, may I show you around?", which often results in the client saying "just looking". If you offer them or their kids a root beer float, you are given a great opportunity to start a conversation. As you walk to the freezer, scoop the ice cream, and ask the big questions like, "Where are you from?" Getting them to converse is key to beginning a relationship.

4. We Collect Information:

I am always frustrated by the agent that tells me they are going to hand out 10 cards that day. That is never the goal. The goal should be to collect 10 cards or 10 potential clients' contact information. During an open house, remember to always have a way to collect their information. A raffle or drawing is always a great way to collect that information.

5. *Strike While the Iron is Hot:*

When I say to get back to the client immediately, it is because we need to strike while the iron is hot. Remember that urgency is the key to sales. I have seen agents not get back to clients until the next day or even a few days later. Clients will move on if they don't get immediate service. At the open house, when your intuition tells you that they are ready to buy now, I always suggest to agents that they have the prospective client grab a Starbucks to kill time so that the agent can wrap up the open house and show them a few homes immediately.

6. Syndicate your Open House:

Post the open house online in the Multiple Listing Service (MLS) or other syndication avenues. By syndicating, this uses your MLS relationships to send out and maximize the exposure to other online mediums. Also, post an invite on your social media, and include a picture (with you in it) to remind everyone of what you do and that you're actually working that day and available.

7. Maximize your Downtime:

During the downtime at the open house, you should still be working. While you may want to sit on the couch and watch a football game, read a romance novel, or riffle through your client's sock drawer, you should be focusing on making the most of this time. So, unless it is Super Bowl Sunday, I suggest you text people from your PCP who live in the area and let them know you are working a local open house. Invite them over and let them know that you are happy to make them a root beer float if they swing by!

8. Don't Short your Open House Time:

With all the work and preparation that goes into creating an open house, I am always surprised when an agent sits an open house for 3-4 hours. A typical workday is generally 6-8 hours, not 3-4. You will triple the attendance by lengthening your open house from 10-4, instead of the lazy open house hours of 11-2. Setting up can be a pain in the arse. Make the most of it.

9. Rainy Days and Holidays Shouldn't get you Down:

What people don't realize is that a buyer willing to look at property on a rainy day or holiday is a motivated one. The buyer that comes to your open house during inclement weather, is worth 5 buyers wandering through on a sunny non-holiday.

These are just a few of the basics for lead generation, but should never be underestimated. From the new agent to the veteran agent, you will find these lead generation tools and techniques are a part of every successful arsenal. In conclusion, branding, being social, and the open house will never go out of style and will always produce positive financial results.

COMMANDMENT 3

Become an Online Rockstar

Generally, the themes discussed so far deal with our social interaction in real life (as the kiddies say). The same, basic rules apply to our social media and online interactions. It is amazing how much of our lives we spend online today. I consider myself to be up on current events, and yet I have not purchased a newspaper or magazine subscription in over 15 years.

With Al Gore's invention of the internet and the convenience of smart phones, like most people, I now get the majority of my news (and fake news) online. When I am looking to buy a car, I don't buy an Autotrader magazine or the

Recycler, I look on Craigslist. When I am purchasing books, clothes, or even small household items, I always look on Amazon first. And, it is estimated that when it comes to real estate, nearly 90 percent of all real estate consumers are looking online for properties before they ever contact an agent. Thus, it is no mystery where our business is headed.

On the bright side, your online persona is generally created, controlled, and promoted by you. You get to develop your message. With the power of the major online search engines and your ability to create your own profile, your online presence can turn you into a superstar agent. There are a select few agents who have this process down to a science. However, most agents (probably 95 percent), don't even know where to begin. My goal in this section is to provide you with a few SIMPLE steps to help you build a powerful online real estate persona.

Step 1. Make Time to Cultivate your Online Brand

Your online brand, which can be a nickname, phrase, or characterization, is your personal signature on all of your online platforms. This personal signature needs to be uniform, memorable, and catchy. Your brand will definitely give you an advantage over someone who just uses their picture and name. It is well worth your time to brainstorm and create your personal brand.

Step 2. Have a complete Online Persona and Profile

Although online platforms are often changing, at this time, there are generally 6 online profiles that you need to manage: your business

LinkedIn account, Google, Zillow, or your Franchise or Company profile (if applicable), Yelp business page, and of course, Facebook (both personal and business page).

The important thing to remember, when it comes to these online platforms, you need to have a complete profile. Given that there are over 300,000,000 people in the U.S.A., if a client is researching you, they don't want to spend all day trying to find you. Make it easy for potential clients to find you online (a current and recognizable photograph helps).

It is also important to have your contact information readily visible, including your email address and cell phone number. It always amazes me how many profiles I have reviewed (especially on LinkedIn) that do not include the agent's cell phone number.

One last tip, for a telephone number, only include your cell phone number so your client doesn't get lost in the shuffle by calling your office. They might give up trying to reach you.

Step 3. Manage your Reviews

When it comes to reviews, they can be as powerful as a personal recommendation. For instance, with Uber, when you make a request for a vehicle, the driver can see your rating as a passenger. If you are wondering why your Uber driver never shows up, now you know why, you're a 2-star A-hole.

Personally, whenever I am considering a purchase on Amazon, I always choose the product with the highest number of positive reviews. Many times, I will take the time to actually read 4 or 5 reviews. I am even willing to pay a little more for products with higher reviews, as they give me comfort that I am more likely to be satisfied with that product. Real estate buyers and sellers are doing the same thing.

Your online reviews can often be more important than you're listing presentation. Why? If you don't have online reviews available, you may never even get invited to the listing appointment.

Because online reviews are so important, you need to set aside a time each week on your business calendar to contact your clients and ask them to provide you with a review. Positive and numerous reviews will help sell your services to potential clients more than anything else.

Most of the time, if you don't request client reviews, then only the bitter and upset clients will make one. It is your job to be preemptive.

It is your job to build a robust and powerful presence and focus on your online review section for all of your media platforms. Invite clients to leave a review the week prior to closing before they get focused on the moving process.

Step 4. Manage your Online Information

Most likely, someone out there has done major research on you. I can guarantee you that over the span of your career or maybe your personal life, someone has Googled you. Someone has stalked your Facebook page and viewed all of your Instagram posts. My question is, if I checked your LinkedIn, Instagram, Zillow, and Google account TODAY, what would it tell me about the kind of person you are? And in terms of real estate, would I hire the online persona you're showing the world?"

Step 5. Optimizing Facebook

Although my sons like to refer to me as a dinosaur for being such a staunch supporter and user of Facebook, there is no denying that Facebook is a dominating force in social media. It is estimated that there are well over a billion active Facebook accounts in existence as of today.

Facebook accounts are growing at the phenomenal rate of nearly 20 percent a year. In addition to the massive number of users, the demographics of Facebook represent a slightly older crowd with higher income levels compared to other social media platforms. In my opinion, ignoring the power of Facebook would be a crime. This step will outline some ideas for optimizing your Facebook account.

Facebook is not LinkedIn

Your personal Facebook account will always be more impactful than a Facebook page that people can follow and like. People want intimate details about your life and aren't interested in the "business only" posts from your professional page.

Solidifying your relationship with current clients, and attracting new clients by creating a personal relationship with them through your personal posts, is the magic of Facebook for a real estate agent. It is also important to note that people who only post business-related material will be dropped like a bad habit (Facebook is not LinkedIn, so don't treat it as such). I recommend that you post a minimum of 3 positive, personal posts for every 1 positive, business post.

Create positive posts

It is okay if you need prayers or want to pay homage to a loved one, but people who make negative posts will be dropped as fast as the business-only agent.

Being positive attracts positive!

Be Secure

Given that you are using your personal page for business, too, be aware of the pitfalls. Utilize the security settings on your Facebook account. Don't allow people to tag you and make posts without your approval. In your settings options, you can make sure you review anything before it hits your timeline. There is nothing worse than a picture of you flipping the camera the bird or drooling on yourself after a long night at a wedding reception.

Hit that "Like" Button

It is important to remember that people like to be acknowledged. When people are making a post, they want attention for their deeds, thoughts, or actions. When you ignore their posts, people know. They appreciate the fact that you cared enough to like or comment on their post.

Be tasteful and non-political

Be mindful of liking political or tasteless posts (and lately it has become harder to distinguish between these two). The last thing you want to do is alienate half of your clients because you made a political post. Oh... and never post past 11 p.m., unless it's about the birth of your first child. Nothing that should be posted ever happens after 11, I know from experience.

Have a Great Profile and Backdrop

Obviously, posts are important, but just as important is the look and information on your Facebook profile. Make sure your personal profile picture is clear it's you. When someone clicks on your profile, they need to be able to find you easily and recognize you. Your backdrop is equally important. It needs to give people an idea that you sell real estate.

Your backdrop is the best place to let people know what you do.

Whether it's a company photo, logo, a sold sign, or a picture of your business card, people who view your profile need to immediately recognize that you sell real estate.

Friend Request Every Possible Prospect

When I first moved to the town I live in now, my wife and I slowly visited the restaurants, shops, and taverns. I will never forget the visit to a hole-in-the-wall restaurant. We walked through the door, checked out the environment, ordered a beer, and had a brief conversation with the manager. The cool part, she friend requested both of us before we hit the exit. We now receive notifications for the activities and posts from the establishment. It was a lesson for me, and genius on the manager's part.

By the way, we did end up selling her a house.

Have a Post Schedule

It is also recommended that you plan the exact date and time of your posts. When you create your monthly business calendar, make sure that you align events such as family birthdays, sporting events, or any other activities with a personal post schedule. And, always align your business posts with your calendared business activities such as open houses or networking events.

The Selfie

One last tip, when you are making real estate related posts like an open house, never post a picture of a property without you in it. Posts without people in them are generally snoozers and will get minimal attention. Don't forget the most liked post of all, "A SELFIE"! Especially at open houses.

COMMANDMENT 4

Be the Jetsons, not the Flintstones

Early on in my career, I was mentored by an agent named, John, who took me in and showed me the ways of the force. He taught me the value of hard mailers, from just listed and just-sold cards to writing the perfect magazine ad. HE was the top agent in the company when I started, and I looked up to him as a big brother or uncle.

Since those days, we opened more offices, so I didn't get to spend as much time with John as I used to. In 2016, I heard through the grapevine that John had just taken a $1,000,000-plus listing. I was very happy for him as this a rare property in our market place. About 2 weeks later, I heard the seller was cancelling the listing.

I stopped by the office to visit John, only to find that the seller was cancelling the million-dollar listing. When I asked John why, he said the seller wanted to work with an agent who was more tech savvy.

When John went to meet with the seller and get the cancellation signed, I asked him to bring David and Sandy, a couple both in their thirties, who are considered by many, the most "tech" savvy agents. My goal was to encourage the seller to stay with our company by joining David and Sandy's tech skills with John's personal relationship. David attended the meeting with the home owner with John, and was able to retain the listing because of his tech heavy-listing presentation.

When they returned to the office, I excitedly asked David about his presentation. He explained that the tools he uses in his listing presentations are generally the same things available to all agents. He leveraged the locations the MLS syndicates his listings to (i.e. Zillow, Trulia, Realtor.com, Homes.com and more). He showed the seller their personal website, complete online profiles (such as Zillow and Realtor.com), their number of Facebook friends, and general social media reach. Aside from presenting the listing on an iPad, that was it.

David and Sandy retained the million-dollar listing for John by doing nothing more than highlighting the tools that are available and free to most every real estate agent in the country who has an MLS membership.

Highlighting those tools that John already knew about, but did not share with his seller, nearly cost John a high-dollar listing. Luckily, David was able to reel that seller back in. And by the way, by embracing technology, in the last month, David, Sandy, and their team opened 30 escrows. They have leveraged technology and made it their #1 money-making tool!

What are some of the best tech tools available today?

If you ask me, there are currently 3 great tools that everyone should be using to capture potential buyers and sellers. These tools include seller-lead websites, buyer-lead websites, and open-house guestbooks. Although they may soon be passé, for now, they are a popular medium and can make you truly look like a Jetson.

The Seller-lead Website

Have you ever been wandering through Facebook and come across the page that has an ad: "What is your Home Worth?". It's generally a picture of the city you live in (as the backdrop) with a small box for the consumer to enter their address. This is a great seller capture tool.

Through the Elevated Network platform or whatever system you use, a potential client is immediately provided with a list of comparable sales and a market analysis. By spending a few dollars to boost a post or sponsor a post on Facebook, you can capture numerous potential sellers' contact information. You have found a POTENTIAL SELLER! Now follow up!

The Buyer-lead Website

Much like the seller-lead site, the buyer-lead site also uses the power of social media to fish for potential buyers. Just like the seller-lead site, the buyer exchanges their contact information for data. Upon request, buyers are provided an automatic link to the offered data or service. Although used often on social media and perhaps a little overplayed, this is a still a great tool for securing contact information though data capture.

Open House Guestbook

One of my Agents was ranting and raving last weekend that he had over 100 groups through their open house. He said he had over 60 people sign in on 5 separate pieces of paper. Paper? That is truly antiquated in the world of open houses today. There are hundreds of online tools that capture potential client data on a mobile device.

Not only do they capture data and import them into your client pool, they also have auto response texts and emails which get back to the clients at a chosen time.

In Summary

Whatever you do with your digital presence, just make sure that you have one. Let your clients and potential customers know (on social media) that you are up on the latest technology. Let them see "some form of media" produced by you with your picture and branding. Remember, perception is everything. If you do a few things to gain digital visibility, it may be the difference between appearing tech savvy or becoming obsolete.

Be the Jetsons, not the Flintstones.

COMMANDMENT 5

Turn Strangers into Clients

Being social and embracing those tools are key, but we must know the secrets of turning that stranger into a lifelong client.

Creating a Magnetic Attraction

Have you ever noticed that successful agents can bring up the entire energy of the room when they walk in? It's like they turned on a light switch. Often, you can't explain it, but you feel a positive energy and start to get a feeling of excitement when they are around you. It is like they have this innate and powerful magnetic attraction. I want to engage these people and immediately feel an urge to speak with them in the hope that some of their energy will rub off on me.

When I talk about the idea of becoming a successful and financially independent person, this magnetic persona is exactly what needs to be duplicated. And I will let you in on a little secret, you can have that same magnetic draw. It is a universal force.

As we already discussed, positivity is one of the major keys. People are generally drawn to positive people. Just as important, is the level of "energy and enthusiasm" that these personalities carry. Just like positivity being contagious, energy and enthusiasm are also infectious. When you talk to a magnetic personality, without noticing it, your energy level also rises.

Remember People's Names

How many times have you met someone and couldn't t remember their name? When it has happened to me, the conversation always becomes very awkward. It is embarrassing when you have to refer to someone as "buddy" just because you can't recall their name. It is also the ultimate insult.

Don't forget, every person you meet is a potential client, and we need to treat them as such. Here are three basic tools we can use to help remember people's names, and in so doing, increase the size of our potential client pool.

1) Always **ask them to repeat their name** after they say it… "I'm sorry, what was your name again?"
2) When you're talking to them, **immediately reuse their name** when you address them.

"So, Jason, how long have you lived in the area?"

3) **Find some feature** that is unique to them while you associate the name. (e.g. Barbara Brown eyes).

This is the most basic tool to starting a relationship. But at a deeper level, remembering their spouse or children's names can be 20 times more powerful. One of my close friends who is very successful in medical sales says "the key to building relationships begins with remembering the name and some details about the front-office receptionist". Remembering their name is first, but remembering their children's name and whatever they are involved in is relationship gold.

Leverage your Social Media

Social media is an extremely powerful tool to build meaningful relationships. I received a call from the president of the world's largest real estate company while on the road one day. The first question he asked me was, "Your son seems to be doing great in football, do you think they may actually win state?" I was dumbfounded that he knew such personal information about my son. I was also flattered that he was interested in what was going on in my life.

After a few minutes I realized that he had jumped on my Facebook account to see what was happening with me before our call. I was impressed, and immediately felt like he cared about me. That is a good lesson for all of us, and explains how he earned his post as president.

Remember to always make the conversation about *them*. No offense, but nobody wants to hear you talk. In general, everyone is more interested in hearing themselves speak. It drives me crazy when I walk by a conference room and there is one agent droning on without allowing the client to talk.

In my experience, if an agent is talking for 20 minutes without listening, generally, they are doomed. Remember, if you are talking, you are not learning about your clients, and are not building a relationship with them.

Asking questions is one of the best ways to create that magnetic draw. Try to remember this when you catch yourself talking too much, **SHUT UP AND LISTEN!**

The 6 Keys to Building Powerful Relationships

1) Remember to always **stay positive**, energetic, and enthusiastic.

2) Always **connect** with people at a deeper level than the superficial hello.

3) Take an interest in people by **remembering the simple things** like their names and something unique about them or their family.

4) Social media can be a powerful tool to open dialogue with anyone. **Look at their profile before you meet.** If it was important enough for them to post, it is something they would "love" to talk about.

5) Ask questions that open the door for them to talk about themselves and then, **SHUT UP AND LISTEN!** People don't want to hear you talk, they want to hear themselves talk. Also, when they are talking, actively listen, they may be

saying something that you want to remember for the future.

6) Finally, ALWAYS REMEMBER!! Find a way to **remind them that you sell real estate**.

COMMANDMENT 6

Create Clients for Life

An agent's success in real estate is dependent on how effectively they can build and cultivate a loyal and deep **PCP.** An agent's A+ PCP should be a list of the 100 people they know and believe would consider using them for their real estate needs. An agent's PCP should contain the complete contact information for these 100 or so people. Most of the time, new agents are hesitant to solicit business from people they know (this is a mistake).

We've all had that awkward (perhaps horrible) experience with a friend or family member that joined a multi-level marketing company and pressured us to attend their cookware, jewelry, or make-up party. However, as real estate agents, **we must engage our friends and family** and overcome our fears that we will be unwelcome or seen as pests.

Successful agents will immediately tell you, "start by building you're A+ PCP Top 100. You need to engage and solicit business from everyone you know, including friends and family. If you are not willing to do that, perhaps you should start looking for another career."

When I do an interview with an agent who is new to the business, I can generally tell within 15 minutes whether their career will be an uphill battle, or if it has the potential to take off like a rocket. For example, when I interview someone who just moved to California from Wisconsin, I know real estate may be a difficult road for them, as they have no local contacts or community reputation. As a result, their PCP may be limited.

Now compare that to the person who is currently serving as their local homeowners association community events director, or who also serves as the treasurer of the local elementary school PTA. If that agent plays their cards right, they are destined for financial greatness as their PCP is already deep.

Creating your Potential Client Pool

When a new agent joins our organization, I make sure they create a robust PCP as soon as possible. As we discussed, depending on how long they have lived in the area, we generally set out an attainable number to begin with, between 40 and 100 people.

It's not just about identifying A+ people, but about gathering all their modes of communication. Just a name and phone number is not enough. We need complete information for each contact on our list.

That includes name, spouse, address, cell phone number, email, and social media contacts (e.g., Facebook and LinkedIn). And this is just the bare minimum. As discussed under the Turning Strangers into Clients Commandment, knowing things like people's birthdays, the names of their kids, and their interests, can help you maximize and personalize your relationship with them.

Often, the first step in creating a PCP will also result in generating immediate business. If you are like me, your phone contains a ton of people's contact information, which has been added over the years. So, unless you have just dropped your phone in a toilet without backing up your information to the cloud, your personal phone is a goldmine for your PCP.

Each of the contacts in your phone are people who have some form of a relationship with you. When you reach out to them, this is a great opportunity to not only develop your PCP, but can open the door to a discussion about their current real estate needs. In turn, this could result in a listing or sale. Thus, I recommend all agents reach out to each person in their phone contacts with a text.

Example Initial Text:

> *Hi Art, this is Chuck. I am updating the contact information on my favorite people. Could you please text me your email and home address? Thanks again, and say hi to Karen and the boys for me. BTW, don't forget me if you ever have any real estate needs!* ☻

Notice this text is personal. It indicates the name of the contact and refers to their spouse or significant other. Never send this text in a group or without mentioning their name directly (remember, these contacts may be your "friends and family"). Although you may not get an immediate response, don't be discouraged. Remember, everyone is busy, but eventually they will get back to you. Hopefully with a listing!

Once you have exhausted your telephone contacts, the second way to reach out to your clients is through Facebook. A private Facebook message should be sent to everyone that you think may use you for their real estate needs. Remember to keep a list of who and how you have contacted people, you don't want to send a Facebook message to the same people you text. Also, there are many people who are not following up on their Facebook messages, so, again, don't feel bad if people don't respond.

Here is an example of a simple message:

> *Hi Pete, I know we are Facebook friends, but I don't have your cell number or home address. I was hoping to catch up sometime. Hope everything is great with you and Emily! Talk to you soon! BTW, don't forget me if you ever have any real estate needs.* ☺

Now that you have reached out through a text or Facebook, you can do the same with a phone call or email depending on what contact details you have for them. Reaching out through these mediums to build your PCP puts you WAY AHEAD OF THE COMPETITION! A current and actively worked A+ PCP sets you on a path to a long and successful career in real estate.

Don't assume that everyone you know is aware of what you do for a living. For example, during my last year coaching my son's football team, I learned a lesson from Kurt, one of my assistant coaches. We had been coaching together for nearly 3 years. After practice, as we were walking across the field, he asked what I did for a living. I told him that our company sells homes. I will NEVER forget his response. He said, "you're kidding! I just listed my house last Sunday. I wish I would have known".

In shock, the real estate agent in me was taken aback and felt like a complete failure. Remember, as an agent, you have a responsibility to scream from the mountaintop to everyone you know, "I SELL HOMES". My second error was that I never added Kurt to my client pool. Let me tell you, that conversation hurt!

How do you use your PCP once created? What is the balance between overselling to friends and family, and just being there for them? This is a balancing act we must all keep front and center in our minds. As real estate agents, if we are too timid, we will be overlooked and our friends and family may unknowingly use someone else for their real estate needs.

For those who are not from the local area or have not had the time to be as social or involved in the local community, don't be discouraged. It is now time to start putting yourself out there, so you can begin to use and expand your PCP. It doesn't matter whether your PCP is big or small, it is how you use it, as they say.

As mentioned in Commandment 1, Become a Walking Talking Billboard, as a "new to area" real estate agent, it is important to remember that your job is to attend every single social and public event you possibly can.

In this business, "Who you know and who you meet is everything." The goal is to put you and what you do in front of the people you meet as often as possible.

Generally, the successful agent is not the one who is the shy or introverted type. Most of the time, **success comes to the loud and proud agent**!

As mentioned earlier, I generally recommend no more than 100 of your best A+ contacts should be in your primary PCP. What do I mean by best contacts? Every person over the 100th contact in your primary PCP should be carefully considered. Ask yourself who in your PCP is LESS likely than the new contact to use you for their real estate needs or to refer you. Move anyone less likely to contact you to your secondary client list. This keeps your primary PCP as the VIPs in your fan club.

COMMANDMENT 7

Embrace the Power of Personal Relationships

In order to be successful in real estate sales you need to create "clients for life". Those clients who will use you for their real estate needs again and again. How do you create clients for life? Although it sounds cliché, keeping in contact with your clients on a personal level is the best way. Without nurturing long term personal relationships, you run the risk of finding out that the house you sold to the cute couple two years ago was just listed and sold by someone else.

"If you don't keep in contact with your past clients, how can they ever be your future clients?"

We spend day after day working in the real estate sales business trying to find leads. We are constantly mining every avenue of our lives trying to find that person interested in buying or selling property. Once we have found them and sold them a home, how do we make sure they will use us again and recommend us to their friends and family? We can't be like the used car salesman or the single ladies' man agent in your office (you know who you are). Remember, "you can't take the hit-it-and-quit-it attitude with clients". Reputable studies have shown that **acquiring a new customer can cost as much as 25 times more than retaining an existing one**.

If you recall from the beginning of this book, my first sale was to a young couple (Dan and Heather) who were both 24-years-old when they wandered into the real estate office. They were married less than a year and were expecting their first baby in 5 months. At the time of their first purchase, they were just getting started in their careers and were in the $250,000 starter home market. Since that day (twenty years ago), I have gone on to sell them 7 houses over the years, and listed and sold 5 for them.

That is twelve sales over this twenty-year relationship. Also, I have sold both of their parents' homes and countless other friends and family that they have referred to me.

Most recently, I helped them purchase a home that was valued over $1,000,000. As their lives changed, more children came and their incomes increased. I have been fortunate enough to assist them with their real estate needs all along the way. These sales were not a fluke, but a direct result of my Personal Touch Marketing approach that the VIPs in my PCP receive.

The sales quote we should all live by:

"Your clients don't forget about you, they think you forgot about them ...and why should they reward you for that with business?"

I first learned about Personal Touch Marketing from my partner, Margaret. When I started in real estate, she was the top agent in our local board of real estate and had been for years. I will never forget the day when I saw her loading her car with cheesecakes to deliver to her top clients on Thanksgiving.

On other occasions, I saw her mailing handwritten personal notes to her clients for their birthdays. She is the most considerate and caring agent that I have ever met. Most of her clients begin their meetings with a hug.

Her approach is to take a genuine interest in her clients, and to not forget about them once the deal was done. The following are some Personal Touch Marketing ideas that successful agents use.

Items of Value and Thoughtfulness

There are so many things that you can send your clients throughout the year that they will appreciate and enjoy. For instance, the type of things you can send your clients are: See's Candy around the holidays, a personal note with a lottery ticket for St. Patrick's Day, or a branded beach ball for Memorial Day. Whenever you send these types of items, it reminds them you are there for their real estate needs and have not forgotten about them.

I can think of no better example of the power of sending out these thoughtful gifts than what happened to me during my fourth year of real estate. I was a young and up and coming agent trying to expand my client pool. One day I received a listing call from a high-profile musician living in my area that I had met once in person and added to my PCP. At the meeting, he points to my branded beach ball floating in his pool and says, "You see that beach ball, that is why you are here. I know you are a newer agent and I should probably go with a more experienced one, but there is no way I couldn't use you. You always send me the coolest stuff."

The day after I listed his house, I received a 10-day cash offer from the same agent (from a different office) that had sold him his house three years ago. That was the sweetest part of the whole story.

Personal Client Texts

With the rise of technology, there are also many "free ways" of reaching out to your clients. I am a HUGE fan of the power of texting. If you recall, we initially reached out to grow our PCP via text while building our database. Texting is a great way to reach out to your clients without being too pushy. Through texting, the client does not have to immediately respond and is less likely to feel that you are interrupting or bothering them. In addition, it also helps make sure that clients have your telephone number.

Example Texting Program – Personal:

> *Hi Pete, this is Chuck. I hope everything is good with you and Cathy. I was just thinking about you guys and wanted to wish you a Happy New Year! I saw on Facebook that you just had your first grandson. Congrats! Hope all is well. BTW, don't forget me if you have any real estate needs.* ☺

Rules of Texting:

1) **Their Name**. Never send texts without it being personalized. No group texts.

2) Be sincere, **genuine**, respectful, and appreciative

3) Always include **something personal** and of interest to them specifically

4) Include **your name** and where they know you from.

I guarantee you that these types of texts have more value than any marketing ad or farming mailer you may invest in. Clients that know you care will always be in your corner and can be your best marketing tool.

If you have developed personal relationship with your clients, it is never a problem to directly ask them to help you with your business. Never underestimate the power of "Business Prospecting Texts."

Example Texting Program – Business Prospecting:

Hi Pete, I am texting you with my real estate hat on. I have a client looking for a 4 bedroom in your area. We have seen everything on the market and are not having any luck. Do you know anyone who may be looking to sell? Let me know, and say hi to Kathy. 💤

If I were to just send out business prospecting texts, without laying the personal relationship groundwork, I would begin to be ignored and look like I am only interested in their relationship for business. Just like the agent who only posts real estate posts on Facebook, people will begin to be annoyed by you. Keep it personal, and remember they want to know you care and don't just see them as a paycheck.

There are a million other ways to build lifelong relationships through the personal touch method. These include phone calls, personal notes, face-to-face contact, community events, and client parties. Remember these things are just ideas. You need to choose what personal touch techniques best suit your personality.

Remember to plan out these actions "in advance" and be systematic. We will discuss this further in the next commandment.

COMMANDMENT 8

Become an Action Item Junkie

As I discussed at the beginning of this book, I have been fortunate enough to have had what most people would define as great financial success in this business. But, without a doubt, I have taken the long road. If I could go back and visit myself on my first day in real estate, I wouldn't share any insightful real estate war stories or quotes about having a positive mindset. Instead, I would share the power of an actionable business calendar.

In my 15 plus years of interviewing and hiring prospective agents, I always ask agents making the move to our company to provide me a copy of their business plan. Unfortunately, most agents are coming from companies where their previous brokers have not taken the time or effort to help their agents create a great plan. I believe that doing this is one of the greatest values a broker can bring.

On the rare occasion they actually do have a business plan, it usually includes vague ideas about the agent's value proposition, pie-in-the-sky marketing plans, and dreams about how much money they want to make. In general, my immediate response is to tell the agent to toss this type of business plan directly into the trash can.

Vague and theoretical business plans are not effective. We are in the real estate business, not a freshman philosophy class. To that end, make sure you have a specific and actionable business calendar that you follow every day.

We highly encourage our agents to be action item junkies!

When creating a business calendar, the action items should be specific to each agent's strength and likes. By strengths, we are referring to action items that the agent enjoys doing or at least what the agent is willing to do to grow their business. If an agent absolutely hates door knocking, then their action plan does not reflect knocking on 25 doors a day. Instead, let's say an agent enjoys being social, working with local charities, chambers of commerce, or their kid's sports teams. The agent should focus their actions on scheduling and optimizing these types of social activities instead.

Here is where all the tools we discussed in this book (so far) come into play.

From social media posts, social events, networking opportunities, and open houses, all of our lead generation activities need to be integrated into the action items portion of your business calendar.

However, the first step we need to take is to set aside a specific time each month where we focus on scheduling out our upcoming month. My suggestion is a Friday morning during the last week of the month.

As I mentioned earlier, when we are distracted by transaction problems or issues, we often find excuses and reasons not to accomplish our action items. Because of life and business emer-

gencies, you will inevitably miss a few calen-
dared action items, but **MISSING YOUR
CALENDAR CREATION APPOINTMENT IS NOT AN
OPTION.**

You need to lock yourself away. This is the
most important action to guarantee your focus
stays on creating Leads, Leads and Leads. When
you are completing your calendar, find some
way to avoid distraction.

---

*Shut off your phone, close your email, and pay
your kids to keep away. It won't be easy, but
creating your action item calendar should be
your first and most important priority task
each month.*

Building the Calendar

For me, there is a very specific formula and
prioritized order that needs to be followed when
creating your monthly calendar. Following this

priority list will help you build a successful business, but will also help guide you to success in your life.

If you are not taking care of things at home, I have found it impossible to focus on my business. That being the case, let's start there. My first suggestion is to always focus your calendar on your family, friends, and home life first. This would include things like scheduling upcoming birthdays, anniversaries, church, and date nights. These are the types of things that keep a happy, healthy life and remind us why we work.

Making sure we handle the things that bring life balance is where we should ALWAYS start, but then there is the art of reaching out and building relationships with our clients. Throughout this book are numerous lead-generating activities. Just remember that now we need to quantify how many, what day, and what time. If you have already forgotten, lead generating activities include texting, personal notes, scour- ing social media for leads, open house schedul- scheduling, and networking events.

For example, when you are adding an entry to your calendar that you are going to do 20 seller prospecting texts (asking your PCP if they know anyone who may want to sell), be specific as to the day and time you will be sending those texts. Actions like that will bring you success and money while building on your talents and strengths.

If an action item like texting is not entered in your calendar, it will never get done.

It is also important to make sure that every day you have a prospecting action item (like texting) scheduled. As we have already touched on, time and time again, I have seen agents get themselves into a position where they are so busy being a fireman on their 4 current deals, that they forget to continue to prospect.

Then, a month down the road, these agents have ZERO pending sales and limited prospects. If you take a few hours during the last week of every month to plan out your next month's activities, you are guaranteed not to fall into the ZERO sales trap.

I don't care if it's 10 texts a day or 5 personal notes, you must be specific and commit to an action EVERY DAY, or run the risk your income pipeline running dry. Success can be as simple as spending 10 minutes per day reaching out to your PCP.

An actionable business calendar is a tool that can help you be effective at being your own boss. You must lay out your plan of action on your calendar, and hold yourself accountable to completing these items every day. If you do not have the self-discipline to do this, I suggest working with someone that can help to keep you accountable. This could be your manager, broker, or a real estate coach.

I wish I had figured this out sooner. If I knew the simple recipe of creating a specific and actionable business calendar (and FOLLOWING it), I could have achieved the same level of financial success I have today in 7 years, instead of 20.

To this day, I religiously follow my business calendar. I don't miss appointments like I used to, and I am 100 times more efficient than when I first started in the business.

COMMANDMENT 9

Refine your Goals and Create your Fuel

Many people who join the real estate industry are coming from a career where they had a boss or supervisor who was in charge. The reason that the boss is the boss is that they generally have a vision of what needs to get done, the authority to move forward, and an understanding of the organization's goals.

Basically, the boss has experience and information that the employee "worker bee" does not. They know how many units they need to move, how much revenue they must create, and an understanding of the plan of how to get there. The successful real estate agent must be armed with the same information as it pertains to their individual real estate business. Now that we are on our own, independent and responsible for ourselves, the worker bee mentality will no longer cut it.

Now that we are the business owner and operator that we always wanted to be, we have to put on multiple hats to be successful. We have to be the accountant, CEO, motivational sales manager, administrative secretary, and the personal assistant.

The only way we can stay focused is to always be aligning our actions to our big-picture goals. Goals are what give us the motivation to ask the big questions. What is my motivation? What am I trying to accomplish? Basically, why do I work?

Creating your personal, material, and financial goals

For me, I get up each day, focus and refocus on my personal goals. I have been fortunate in my life and feel an obligation to "pay it forward" by encouraging everyone around me to reach their full potential. Inherent in my goals is my "WHY". As an owner, broker, and trainer, I know what gives me satisfaction in life. The thought of someone not making it in my organization, or changing companies because I did not provide value, makes me crazy. I feel responsible for people around me and their success. It gets me motivated, even on the days when I am not feeling it.

I would ask you to take some private time to determine your "Why". What is your motivation for being successful? Is it because you have a family to take care of? Is it because you grew up poor and never wanted your children to deal with the same struggles? Do you have a hot spouse that you want to make sure you keep happy? Whatever the reason, **you need to write it down**. Below is a quick outline of how I determine what is important for me. I usually break these down into 3 categories which include personal, material, and economic/financial goals. I've also included a few examples of personal development goals to help provide you with a framework to do your own.

Personal Development Goals

Personal Development Goals	Why do I want it?	What is your 1st Action Item?	Life Priority
Learn to play guitar	*Childhood Goal*	*Google a teacher*	6
Visit my Mom monthly	*She is getting older*	*Set time with Mom*	3
Take wife to Hawaii	*Been promising for years*	*Check Expedia*	4
Get down to 180lbs	*Energy for kids and grandkids*	*Get gym membership*	2
Take a family vacation	*Family bonding and memories*	*Check Expedia*	1
Get cleaning lady	*More free time*	*Find one*	5

* Your blank worksheet is in the back of the book

It is a relatively simple process. I would begin by asking you to choose your most important personal goals for the next year. Let's say the first is to "learn to play piano", second may be "a family vacation", and so on. Once you have listed all of your personal goals (not material or financial goals), we must ask ourselves "Why are they important?" Let's say in this case, you want to make sure that you maintain communication with your children and let them experience things that they have never seen. And, what is the first action you must do to make this happen? Look on Expedia and see the cost to hold a spot for this vacation. Then, you move through and complete the entire sheet. Lastly, you have to determine the priority of these goals. List out the priority on the far-right column. All of the sudden, you have set your personal development goals for the next year. **Now go get them!**

In terms of material goals, I have given some examples of things that may be of interest for you. Something that has been on your list, something that you work for, keeps you motivated. I have also given some examples of the "WHY", action items and priorities. Take a few minutes to review these examples and lay out your material goals over the next year.

Material Goals

Material Goals	Why do I want it?	What is your 1st Action Item?	Life Priority
New Car	Because I work hard	Figure out payment	3
Rolex	Lifelong Goal	Get picture on goal board	4
Louis Vuitton Purse	Something for just me	Pick one and price it out	6
Pool	More family time	Get estimate	2
Remodel Kitchen	I want to love my home	Sketch it up	5
Mommy Makeover	Feel good about me and hubby	Get a price	1

* Your blank worksheet is in the back of the book

Now that your personal development and material goals have been determined, you need to determine your economic and financial goals.

Economic and Financial Goals

Economic and Financial Goals	Why do I want it?	What is your 1ˢᵗ Action Item?	Life Priority
Monthly expenses under $5,000	Low payments = start saving	Create business calendar	2
$20,000 cash in savings	Safety net 3 months expenses	Create business calendar	3
$2,000 passive monthly income	So I don't have to work forever	Create business calendar	6
$30,000 in college fund	Kids off to college in 5 years	Create business calendar	4
Pay off credit cards	Tired of paying high interest	Create business calendar	1
Buy a rental	I want to retire someday	Create business calendar	5

* Your blank worksheet is in the back of the book

Congratulations! For some of you, this may be the first time you have set out personal, material, and financial goals. Since my first few years in the real estate business, my friends and I have always locked ourselves away for a few days to work directly on our goals and plans. Whether you do business planning and goal setting with your broker, your mastermind of friends, or some other real estate trainer, it should NEVER be neglected.

Goals are the fuel that keep your engine running, keep you motivated, and remind you of your purpose. Remember to keep your goal tank full.

COMMANDMENT 10

Live and Breathe your Numbers

The millionaire sales agent can always rattle off their year-to-date unit count at the drop of a hat. They can also tell you how many they are trying to attain and will generally know exactly how much money their unit count will equate to.

You should always begin your year by determining your financial goals and the unit requirements needed to reach them. Provided is the exact exercise the agents in our real estate company use. Once your financial goal is determined, we will break the financial goals down to the exact number of transactions you will need to reach your goals. Below you will find an example of step 1.

Annual Financial Planning

Simplifying your Financial Goals	
$ 6,000	What is your financial comfort level?
$ 2,000	How much additional to reach your desired lifestyle?
$ 1,500	Contribution to retirement and savings
$ 9,500	TOTAL Monthly income goal
Monthly Goal $9,500 x 12 (months) = **$114,000 Annual Goal**	

* Your blank worksheet is in the back of the book

In the above example, to live the life for this agent, they will need $114,000 per year. Now, take a few minutes to run through this exercise for yourself. Even if you use a rough estimate, it is a start.

Now that you have determined your own annual financial goals, we need to figure out how many transactions it will take you to get there. Before we go any further, I would ask that you take a few minutes to estimate your annual real estate costs. Here is a rough example of some things to consider when working up your expenses.

Annual Expense Estimate

$ _____	Desk / monthly office fees
$ _____	Cell phone
$ _____	Internet and wifi
$ _____	Mileage & auto expenses
$ _____	Office supplies
$ _____	Computer hardware
$ _____	Software expenses (Office 365, MS Word??)
$ _____	CRM subscriptions (Elevated Network)
$ _____	Education and license renewal
$ _____	Seminars, events, and conventions
$ _____	Purchasing leads (Zillow, Homes.com, etc…)
$ _____	Hard mailers and postage
$ _____	Flyers and brochures
$ _____	Videography and photography
$ _____	Yard signs, open house signs, business cards
$ _____	Website, domain renewal and hosting
$ _____	Print ads (magazines, phone book, paper, etc…)
$ _____	Professional and legal (CPA/Lawyer)
$ _____	Assistants (salary, bonus, and benefits)
$ _____	License renewal and fees
$ _____	E&O insurance
$ _____	Medical, disability insurances
$ _____	Charitable donations and sponsorships
$ _____	Banking fees and checks
$ _____	Payroll service
$ _____	Corporate costs
$ _____	Coaching
$ _____	Other _____
$ _____	Other _____
$ _____	Other _____
$ _____	**TOTAL EXPENSES**

* Your blank worksheet is in the back of the book

Remember that I'm not a Certified Public Accountant, and there are always changes to the tax laws. Please check for yourself as to what is tax deductible and what is not.

Now that you have your "Total Expenses", you can move on to step 2. Step 2 is what I call the financial goal formula.

Financial Goal Formula

Annual Financial Goal Amount (from above)	$ 114,000
Annual Real Estate Expenses (from above) (+)	$ 5,000
(a) Revised goal amount	$ 119,000
	$ 7,000
(b) What is your average net per deal? (ask your broker)	
(a) $119,000 / (b) $7,000 =	**17 Transactions**

* Your blank worksheet is in the back of the book

Now take into account that you will probably need an additional 4 deals just to pay your income taxes. So, make sure you revise your 17 transactions and add 4 (for taxes), for a total of 21 transactions for the year. Remember, put money away for taxes.

NOW YOU HAVE THE ALL-IMPORTANT, ANNUAL TRANSACTION GOAL!!!!

COMMANDMENT 11

Have a Winning Mindset and Persona

If you have taken the time to complete the goals and numbers set out in Commandments 8, 9, and 10, you are well on your way to winning the real estate game. The value of chasing down leads should be more apparent than ever.

And, most likely, you are a little taxed from those exercises. I implore you, hang in there! We are going to talk about how to help you reach your maximum potential in this real estate sales game.

The only way to reach our maximum potential is to develop a winning real estate sales mindset that exceeds those of our competing realtors.

Not all of us can play guitar like Eric Clapton, interview like Oprah Winfrey, or throw a football like Brett Favre. What we can do, is make the most of our God-given tools, talents, and circumstances, and create our own success recipe.

Success comes when opportunity meets preparation and we decide to start embracing the talents, strengths, and circumstances that we are blessed with. To do that, we must take inventory of our current circumstances and create a clear vision of "who and where we are" and "who and where we want to be".

How do "YOU" Define Success?

Working with successful agents, I have found that the key to creating a winning mindset and attitude is to first determine how "you" personally define success. When you take the time to define your version of success, you begin to identify who you are and who you need to be to get there.

As you determine your version of success, I encourage you to look past financial success alone. Although financial success shows a high level of business achievement, I can save you the suspense, money will not buy you happiness (but it will buy you a Mercedes Benz to drive to places that make you happy). Real success comes from the positive impression and impact we make on the lives of our family, friends, peers, and clients.

What is a "Personal Persona"?

A personal persona can best be defined as the way people that you interact with would describe you. When I ask my agents how their last client would describe them, some of them have horrified looks on their faces. Others are very enthusiastic about how their clients would describe them. As agents, we need to be mindful of the personal persona we project out to our clients and the world.

Think about how you would describe the personal persona of the most successful people you know. My guess is that the people you are thinking of share similar characteristics and traits such as high energy, innate drive, and enthusiasm. It is not a coincidence; it is a calculated formula that breeds success. Thus, your personal persona is the mindset and attitude that you carry around with you each day.

Once you understand what success means to you, and you know your own personal persona, it's time to embrace that understanding and make it your reality. Much like the Buddhist monks who consistently chant the mantra that reinforces their belief system, we must do something similar, just not as extreme as wearing a robe at the top of 5000 steps.

In many ways, this mantra equates to what many people would call "positive affirmations". These positive affirmations embody your definition of how to create the mindset and attitude you need to reach the level of success we all desire.

Exercise: Creating your Personal Persona Mantra

In my opinion, there is no more important exercise than determining our specific personal persona. We need to start by asking ourselves the following questions:

1) How would those closest to me (my friends and family) describe me?

Exercise 1:

Now take a minute to describe in a few words, what you would like them to say.

I want my family and friends to describe me as:

Caring and concerned about them
A good example
Compassionate

* Your blank worksheet is in the back of the book

2) In a perfect world, how would my clients and peers describe me?

Exercise 2:

Now take a minute to describe in a few words, what you would like them to say.

I want my clients and peers to describe me as:

Knowledgeable
Reliable
Trustworthy

* Your blank worksheet is in the back of the book

3) What type of tasks should I do daily?

Exercise 3:

Now take a minute to describe how you can stay positive and project a positive attitude.

The positive actions I need to take daily are:

Always be looking for opportunities
Pay someone a compliment
Always be encouraging

* Your blank worksheet is in the back of the book

Now, take the top answers from each of the above questions and try prioritizing them into a five or six-line summary. This list provides you with your personal persona mantra, which you need to follow to reach your desired level of success. Next, you need to post and re-affirm your personal persona mantra daily.

My Personal Mantra

I will motivate, inspire, and lead by example!
I will search out and find new opportunities!
I will avoid negative and unhealthy thoughts!
I will surround myself with positive people!
I will focus on God's "big plan" for me!
I will encourage others to reach their full potential!

* Your blank worksheet is in the back of the book

Just as important as the creation of your personal persona mantra, is where and how you display it. I would take a few minutes to consider, **where is your thinking place?** For me, my thinking place is in the shower. Every morning when I wake up, I have always formulated my thoughts and determined what I need to accomplish daily in the shower. It's the only place I know I can be alone with my thoughts. Perhaps it's because my two sons never want to bother dad in the shower. But with that knowledge, I had my mantra carved into a granite plaque which hangs in my shower.

For me personally, my mindset has greatly improved since I created and posted my mantra. My newly reinforced attitude has helped to subconsciously move me forward with many, if not all of the goals I set out for myself. Proof of my mantra driving my results is the book you are reading right now. This book is a direct result of the right mindset and attitude, and the goal that I set to share these thoughts with anyone who may find them useful.

CONCLUSION

Begin your Personal Real Estate Journey!

Everything that has occurred in your career and life have sculpted you into a "full-of-potential real estate salesperson". Things like your gender, mentors, education, and geography are all unique to you. Each of us are special in our own way with our own set of personal experiences and tools. For each of us, a plan was set out from the day we were born to bring us right to where we are today.

And yes, some of your life's rollercoaster rides have been difficult and scary. Unfortunately, life is not always a party.

There will be great successes in your life, but there will also be difficult times when we are faced with adversity. You can allow those times to discourage and weaken you, or you can choose to let them empower you.

It is the hard and difficult times in our lives that teach us life's greatest financial and moral lessons. Often, the lessons which were the most painful, can end up being God's greatest gift.

Although I have had what some would consider a very successful career in real estate, it has not come without some bumps and bruises. For me, my biggest business lesson came from a poor decision I made in 2011. As a result, my broker's license was revoked for 18 months. Imagine that...with a company of over 250 agents, I had to call each and every one and explain my situation. Since that day, my company, attitude, and vision have become stronger than ever.

Although humbling and painful, that experience has made me a better person and put me on a new and inspired path.

Aside from my story, I can guarantee you that the most successful people in the world have dealt with difficult times. From divorces, deaths, illnesses, or financial failures, successful people don't let life's roadblocks stop them. A successful mindset requires that you embrace these experiences and use them as the fuel to motivate and inspire you.

As successful sales agents, it is important to have the right mindset and never take our eyes off our primary goal...creating financial success. And of course, financial success only comes when we have a plan of action and a firm understanding of how we create and cultivate leads.

In conclusion, the 11 Commandments have provided you with a plan and the tools necessary to be a real estate success. Remember, you must always be a walking talking billboard and no one should ever ask "what you do for a living".

We must always focus on lead generating activities like the all-powerful open house. In addition, a tech savvy appearance and rockstar, online persona may be the difference between getting that listing appointment or waiting for your phone to ring. Success comes from creating a powerful potential client pool, keeping your relationships strong, and keeping your business flowing. Your financial future is based on the action items you create in your business calendar and your ability to get them done!

LAST, BUT NOT LEAST, if you embrace and implement the lead-generating tools laid out in the 11 Commandments of Real Estate Sales, you *will* be well on your way to creating your own financial and career heaven.

Creating "Your" Goal Worksheet

Material Goals

Material Goals	Why do I want it?	What is your 1st Action Item?	Life Priority

Economic and Financial Goals

Economic and Financial Goals	Why do I want it?	What is your 1st Action Item?	Life Priority

Personal Development Goals

Personal Development Goals	Why do I want it?	What is your 1st Action Item?	Life Priority

Annual Expense Estimate

$ _____	Desk / monthly office fees
$ _____	Cell phone
$ _____	Internet and Wifi
$ _____	Mileage & Auto Expenses
$ _____	Office Supplies
$ _____	Computer hardware
$ _____	Software expenses (Office 365, MS Word ??)
$ _____	CRM subscriptions (Elevated Network)
$ _____	Education and license renewal
$ _____	Seminars, events and conventions
$ _____	Lead generation purchase (Zillow, Homes.com, etc…)
$ _____	Hard mailers and postage
$ _____	Flyers and brochures
$ _____	Videography and photography
$ _____	Yard signs, open house signs, business cards
$ _____	Website, domain renewal and hosting
$ _____	Print ads (magazines, phone book, paper, etc…)
$ _____	Professional and legal (CPA / Lawyer)
$ _____	Assistants (salary, bonus and benefits)
$ _____	License renewal and fees
$ _____	E & O insurance
$ _____	Medical, disability insurances
$ _____	Charitable donations and sponsorships
$ _____	Banking fees and checks
$ _____	Payroll service
$ _____	Corporation Costs
$ _____	Coaching
$ _____	Other _____
$ _____	Other _____
$ _____	Other _____
$ _____	**TOTAL EXPENSES**

Know "Your" Numbers Worksheet

Annual Financial Planning

Simplifying your Financial Goals	
$ _____	What is your financial comfort level?
$ _____	How much additional to reach your desired lifestyle?
$ _____	Contribution to retirement and savings
$ _____	TOTAL Monthly income goal

Monthly Goal _____ x 12 (months) = _____ Annual Goal

Financial Goal Formula

Annual Financial Goal Amount (from above)	$ _____
Annual Real Estate Expenses (from above) (+)	$ _____
(c) Revised goal amount	$ _____
(d) What is your average net per deal? (ask your broker)	$ _____
(c) $ _____ / (d) $ _____ = 12 Goal	$

Creating Your Personal Mantra

I want my family and friends to describe me as:

I want my clients and peers to describe me as:

The positive actions I need to take daily are:

My Personal Mantra

During Chuck's 20 year career in real estate sales, he has sold nearly $250,000,000 in properties. Chuck currently runs one of the country's largest residential real estate companies and is a national trainer, specializing in real estate technology and agent business planning. He's also the owner/operator of North Star Seminars, Inc. If you would like to book Chuck to speak at your next real estate event, he can be reached at www.NorthStarSeminars.com.